KNOW THE SPIRIT
...the way of the master...

Semisi Pule

CONTENT

Introduction

As we get older, we are increasingly interested in the question of life after death. Our mortality becomes very real as we start counting the years before the finality of death claims us. Are you alright with it? Are you scared? Do you feel its unfair? Would you like to know if there is life after death of the human body?

Most people would rather end life than to live as an invalid or in pain. In fact many governments have approved legislation for euthanasia to be made legal. It will give terminally ill patients, who are suffering and are burdens on their families, an option to die peacefully by their own choice. To rescue some dignity out of their cruel suffering and existence.

It does not give us humans much comfort. We are given no choice. Death is final.

In this ebook, I will discuss some issues and evidence that life does not end with death. That there is another entity that man had often ignored which is there in the background guiding the human and he lives on after the human is dead.

In fact death opens up another new world that we know very little about. Its only because we have not developed our ability to control ourselves and our destiny.

But it is a different existence, not a human body but a Spirit Being takes over our existence after death of the human body.

I have deliberately left out a list of references because it would be easier for readers to google the phrases or topics they wish to read further in order to understand what I am talking about.

Chapter 1.

How do you know the spirit?

We have all had unexplained experiences that sometimes make us wonder. Sometimes in our lives, it seems that somebody else takes over and guide us in what we do or what we become.

Christians attribute this influence to God. What about non-Christians? You may find that there is great similarity among all religions in this aspect.

How does the spirit guide us and why? From observation, there seem to be a condition which must be fulfilled. You must be working towards a good and charitable goal. You must evoke the good

karma of the cosmos, to use a Hindu
expression.

It seems that the spirit requires it.

Example 1.

Suppose you belong to a church, religious
group or working towards the common
good, perhaps a charity.

You plan to do one thing, like play sports
or attend university, but your plan is
smashed to pieces. You are injured and
cannot play sport or you fail to enter
university. You are inconsolable and you
blame everything including God.

But then some years later when your life
turns out to be much better than you
expected or planned, you start thinking.
How did that happen? I did not plan it at
all! It just happened by accident!

You should know, it did not happen by
accident.

You can substitute anything, any plans into this formula and it will still be true. Whatever plans you had that was smashed, it will always turn out better than you expected.

You may be surprised. If you analyze every event and every bad luck or good fortune, in your life, there is always a pattern to it as if somebody is planning it for you.

Guess what the condition is? For life turning out better than you expected?

The condition is your participation in activities for the common good whether it be church, a religion or charitable purpose. I have seen this observation happen in many communities and I believe it is the case.

I would say, I am 100% sure it was God's hand that helped you with your life. It was the Spirit Being that helped you succeed.

What is my evidence?

Start experimenting by using prayer, affirmations or any other non-religious technique to ask your spiritual self to help. You will be surprised when things happen but they may not be always be what you expect. Just like your former plans failing to work, it will be the Spirit Being who will dictate what happens....and you will be shocked and surprised every time.

It will always be for your own good even when you break a bone or feel great pain. Even a disaster maybe a blessing in disguise. We have to understand that the true self is the spirit, not the human. The Spirit Being that is you will dictate what happens and what does not happen.

You may cry from your pain and loss as a human, but it does not change your destiny as a Spirit Being.

Prayer is a form of communication between religious followers and God whether they be Christians, Muslims, Hindus or Buddhists. Prayer is very simple, simply close your eyes and ask God to help you with whatever you want. Closing your eyes does help you concentrate, it also means that you are giving God the wheel to drive your life. You are closing your side and opening God's side.

Christians are the followers of Jesus Christ. Muslims are the followers of the prophet Mohammed. Buddhists are the devotees of Buddha but Hinduism is a general philosophy following many deities.

Christians believe in the Trinity which is 'One God in Three Persons'. God the Father (In Heaven), God the Son (Jesus Christ), God the Holy Spirit.

Christians study the Christian Bible and follow its teachings and moral advise. You may need to study the Christian Bible and faith to understand it, if you are not a Christian.

Affirmations is a non-religious form of asking your 'self' to help. Note affirmations does acknowledge that there is a 'self' or 'person within' which is a powerful entity that can make things happen for you. Affirmations are normally used by followers of 'new age' movements which are not religious, in the Christian sense, but based on Hinduism and other philosophies.

When using affirmations, you simply repeat to yourself what you need to achieve, almost like meditation techniques. Like chanting a mantra.

For example, let's say you are a salesman wanting to sell 20 products and you get a commission of $1,000 from each sale. When you go to an appointment, you sit in your car and prepare yourself and repeat to yourself 1,000 times these words.

'I will sell 20 products today. The customer will welcome my presentation and buy the product from me'

You have already pre-booked the appointments with the customers. You are trying to sell four customers five products each.

The purpose of the affirmations is to first convince yourself that your product is the best and you know that the customers will buy them.

There are many books of this kind of sales technique and the authors say that it works. When you do your presentation after doing your affirmations, the customer can feel your confidence. They can feel your complete faith in your product and they will also have the desire to purchase the product from you.

Affirmations can also be used for other purposes like doing a presentation and convincing yourself that you will do a great job. I believe that the purpose is to persuade the 'self' that your motive is good.

Affirmations can also be used in any other area where you need confidence and 'psyching yourself to succeed' is required.

Why does affirmation work? Is it a product of brain activity? Why does prayer work?

Why do other forms of 'self development' requiring 'developing the self' work?

It is exactly like the stories and evidence published involving NDEs (near death experience) and OBEs (out of body experience).

All the evidence point to the 'self' or what Christians would call the spirit which I often refer to as the Spirit Being because I regard it as a separate entity or rather our eternal soul.... the Spirit Being. We all believe that the soul survives death of the body otherwise why would we have one?

Here's a suggestion to experiencing the spirit in your life ;

1. Pay attention to your surroundings
2. Pay attention to what other people are saying
3. Pay attention to your feelings and thoughts
4. Use prayer to communicate with God
5. Use affirmations to improve your relationship with your Spirit Being.

You may be surprised that you will start feeling and 'knowing' that somebody is talking to you and pointing things out, and helping you in everything you do.

Why do some people get no divine help?

I spoke of the 'condition' in the previous example. The condition that will make everything work for you is that you must be working for the common good or at least try to help others in your own way. Being good yourself. That desire comes from inside, that feeling of philanthropy. The feeling of love towards others allows the 'self' to work for you.

It seems that the 'state of being good or promoter of good' is a pre-condition to your success. That first, you must desire to love others and help them.

It is very interesting that this is very much what Hinduism is about (Buddhism also follow a very similar path). In order to escape the sinful and suffering world, you must do good, so you can return to the Cosmic Spirit or God. You must have good karma to escape the sinful, suffering world.

Example 2.

If you had lost your way and found yourself in a 'destructive situation', the only way is 'out' or 'down'.

When I say 'out', it means death. The only end for you is death because in a destructive life there is no salvation whether by your own actions or others (note this is where Jesus Christ offers salvation for people with destructive lives). Destructive lives include those that rely on substances to give them confidence. Drugs, alcohol, tobacco are examples. This substance use only end in disease and death.

I must say I was a smoker for 30 years and my young 7 year old son told me that the teacher told him smoking is bad. Every time I sit down to have a smoke, the kid comes around and repeat his message as if he is convinced that smoking is bad for me. It occurred to me the kid is right and I just threw the packet of cigarette in the rubbish and never touched another cigarette for 13 years now. I relate this story in one of my ebooks 'Quit smoking in 2 seconds' (amazon.com). One of the immediate advantage, I noticed was a saving of about $30 a week, which I would have spent on cigarettes, I now spent on buying meat and groceries for the family. What motivated the kid to tell me about his teacher at school? I think it was the spirit who motivated the kid so I can spent more money buying him food and other necessities. It touched me really deeply that the little kid does not want to see anything bad happen to his Daddy.

Another amazing story, is my life with alcohol. I drank alcohol for 46 years and it may surprise you that when I started writing this book, I felt a strong message from the spirit that I should also quit alcohol. There are so many programmes on tv with evidence that alcohol does damage the body. I have always convinced myself that alcohol is good for me, and there is evidence that wine maybe good, now I know the spirit does not want me to drink alcohol. Why? Because alcohol is only a treat for the human, it has no bearing on the spirit BUT it does affect the human to the extend that he/she loses control of everything. Just like quitting smoking, I suddenly felt I don't need the alcohol anymore. My view has suddenly changed, I am fully aware of the spirit.

Why does the self let you do it? Let you destroy yourself?

In cases where some people have big disabilities or problems, there is evidence from many accounts that the Spirit Being was in a former life which was destructive too. It does point to the fact that the 'memory' which is stored in the Spirit Being somehow influence the present and the future. The memory of the past destructive life comes to the fore. This is an area where spiritual healing works. It appears that the Spirit Being requires that memory to be corrected.

That is why the Spirit Being does not want me to drink alcohol anymore.

In the case of an American healer, who was neither educated or religious, he often prescribe Christian Bible verses for certain sicknesses. Somehow the Christian Bible verses, usually from the New Testament, helps to correct what is wrong with the patient!

That is evidence that Jesus Christ is who he says he is. God the Son! Otherwise why would the Spirit Being accept the teachings of the New Testament and helps the human to get well?

Going down, is losing everything

When I say 'down', it means that you are just 'sliding down' in the scale of 'good' things and never 'getting anywhere' with your life.

In Christian faith, Christ proposes that you must be good and accept God's will. You must have faith in God's goodness and he will deliver what you need every time. I say need because God may not give you what you want but he will give you what you need.

I have made this observation in many stories I have come across.

In my book, 'Live a Life of Miracles' (amazon.com), I talk about my life too. I suddenly realize that everything that happened against my plans was the work of the spirit....and it turned out better than I expected.

It is the same in all other religions. They practice and believe in the same principle whether they are in Islam, Buddhism or Hinduism. The 3 major religions of the world other than Christianity.

A destructive life would be a life spent on drugs, alcoholism or similar destructive behaviour. Even excessive smoking can cause many health and economic problems in the family.

Incidentally, a life that is like Saul's in the bible could also be termed as destructive. Saul spent all his time planning and scheming against the early Christians. Arresting them for the High Priests of Judaism to be murdered and maimed in the name of the law of those days. Jesus Christ himself was maimed and crucified in the name of that same law.

You may notice that today's laws, in most countries, are much, much better because they are based on the teachings of Jesus Christ.

A destructive life can also include leaders, dictators and people who spent their time destroying others and maiming them.

Idi Amin of Uganda, Hitler of Germany
and even the Romans and their leaders.
What is most interesting is that in many
cases like Hitler and the Caesars of Rome,
they have perfect reasons for what they
do in the eyes of their followers. I have
discussed these issues in my series 'God is
Energy. Do you Believe?', in the case of
Jesus Christ, it was the High Priests of
Judaism and the Romans who crucified
him.

I did talk about Hitler and the Holocaust
in one of my books. I did propose that
Jesus Christ may have used Hitler to
achieve his prophecy. Hitler was a
Christian who persecuted the Jews....but
what is most amazing from that disaster
was the establishment of the State of
Israel in 1948 after World War II.

As I pointed out, the spirit may break
your leg but then you meet the love of
your life in hospital. Coincident? Or the
work of the spirit? Maybe the spirit

wanted that woman for your wife! The spirit knew she is the right one for you.

Did the spirit use Hitler to fast forward the establishment of Israel? To protect the history of Jesus Christ? Why else would it happen? I did propose in my book that God used the Holocaust to ensure the establishment of the guardian of Jesus Christ's history in Israel. Many people might say, 'but that is cruel'. We'll, God did also cause the deluge or flood of Noah which basically killed everything and everybody.

Did God also send the comet which killed off the dinosaurs?

The point, I believe, is that 'the Spirit Being is the true self and the human is just a disposable robot'.

The Crucifixion

In the case of the crucifixion, note, the Roman Prefect of Judaea, Pontius Pilate, did wash his hands off the 'crucifixion of Jesus', he could find no wrong with him in the eyes of Rome. Pontius Pilate is on record to have become a Christian later after the crucifixion of Christ. Who crucified Jesus Christ? The Jews!

Jesus Christ had predicted the fall of Judaism and Jerusalem some 30 years, as recorded in Matthew 24;2, before it actually happened. The historian Josephus Flavius had told the story of the destruction of Jerusalem.

Jesus also predicted the fall of the Roman Empire, the biggest empire the world has ever known.

Jerusalem was totally destroyed by Caesar and the Roman Army. It is said that only the bones of the dead and the sand of the desert that were left after the Roman Army was finished with Jerusalem.

These are very important points in our discussion of the spirit. Firstly, Jesus

Christ already knew some 30 years earlier that the Temple will be destroyed. The most sacred and precious of Jewish possessions.

There is also a record suggesting that Titus Flavius, Commander of the Roman Army, refused the 'laurel of honour' given to him in recognition of his victory in Judea, destroying Jerusalem. He said, that what happened was a 'divine punishment'. What did he mean?

However, the arch of Titus still stands in Rome today.

If you read the account of the destruction of Jerusalem and its Jewish population, it is even worse than the Holocaust. The population, or those that survived the mass murder of the Jerusalem Jews were send to the gladiator arena for the amusement of Rome. Those who were lucky were sold into slavery.

Why did Commander Titus Flavius think it was a divine punishment? Rather than the actions of his army that destroyed Jerusalem?

We know, Jesus Christ already predicted it. He is God the Son and he has the galactic memory of the universe.

Jesus Christ promised his disciples he will send the Holy Spirit to help them. In Acts 2;3, of the Christian Bible, the arrival of the Holy Spirit is described. In my discussions in 'God is Energy. Do you Believe?', I suggest it was the work of the Holy Spirit. It was the Holy Spirit that urged on the Roman soldiers to destroy the temple in Jerusalem against the wishes of Titus, their commander. Why would the soldiers disobey their commander? Isn't it their own thoughts and Spirit Beings in action?

Titus Flavius must have noticed something that made him attribute the destruction of Jerusalem to 'divine punishment'.

The other most interesting observation is that Rome is now the centre of Christianity. Some 2,000 years from when Jesus Christ predicted it when he said to Peter;

'You are the rock and on this rock I will build my church'.

What did Jesus mean? Obviously Peter was the greatest supporter of Jesus. He was the rock of Jesus. Didn't he fight for Jesus when they arrested him? And it did happen Peter was the first Pope of the universal church now known as the Catholic Church. The Vatican is the headquarters of the Catholic church which is the original church started by Jesus Christ and his apostles. Do you believe that the Vatican is God's Kingdom on earth? Like in the Lord's prayer that Jesus taught his disciples?

'Thy Kingdom come, thy will be done on earth'

Jerusalem was destroyed and never rebuilt or recognized for almost 2,000 years.

Here's another interesting observation. The Roman Emperor urged on by his own soldiers became a Christian in the 3rd century AD. The Roman Army helped to spread Christianity around the known world of that time.

Just like the recruitment of Saul, the Roman Emperor Constantine had a vision of Christ who helped him win all his battles. He became the very first Christian Emperor of Rome. It was the most significant development in Christianity. Constantine changed everything in Roman religion, from the old Gods, to honour his new God, Jesus Christ. I would venture as far as suggesting that the Pope's Office was merged with the

Emperor's Office and the Vatican given its mandate.

A home for the Jews

The most mind boggling of all these predictions, just to summarize, by Jesus Christ is the establishment of God's Kingdom on earth. In 1922, the League of Nations recognized the need for a home for the Jewish people after almost 2,000 years of 'exile' (*Note: The Balfour Declaration was a November 2, 1917 letter from British Foreign Secretary Arthur James Balfour to Lord Rothschild that made public the British support of a Jewish homeland in Palestine. The Balfour Declaration led the League of Nations to entrust the United Kingdom with the Palestine Mandate in 1922*).

In 1929, the Vatican was established as a Sovereign Nation after a treaty between the church and the Kingdom of Italy on 11 February of that year. The Vatican is the

smallest country in the world with only
121 acres and 825 people in it.

What does that mean in terms of the
prophecies of Jesus Christ?

It does mean that everything Jesus Christ
predicted has happened, is happening or
will happen.

Jesus Christ taught his disciples to say this
prayer:

Our father which art in heaven
Hallowed be thy name
Thy Kingdom come
Thy will be done on Earth
As it is in Heaven
Give us this day our daily bread
And forgive us our trespasses
As we forgive them that trespass against
us
Lead us not into temptation
And deliver us from evil
For thine is the Kingdom
The power and the Glory

For ever and ever. Amen.

 Do you think that **God's Kingdom** has arrived on earth? It certainly has! What do you think the Vatican is? The Catholic Church is the biggest and oldest Christian Church with almost 2 billion members. It was known as the universal church during the days of the apostles.

Do you think God's will is being done on earth? It certainly is happening.

If you add all the Christians it will be over 4 billion, including people who don't go to church but know about Christ and follow his teachings. It is a very interesting observation that much of the world practice the teachings of Christ yet only a fraction of them go to church regularly.

Is that the will of God? Yes it is. Why? Because it was Jesus Christ himself who pointed out that worshiping God should be done is your heart and in private. You don't need to stand on the street corners and worship God there. Worshiping God is no longer in Jerusalem only or church only, you can worship God anywhere.

There are about 8 billion people on earth in 2021. If you survey all these 8 billion inhabitants whether they have heard of Jesus Christ and his teachings, I would predict that 90% or more of them have. Only the little children in non-Christian countries may not have heard of Jesus Christ.

Is that good? That 10% of the people of the world may not have heard of Jesus Christ?

I believe it does not really matter. Whether you are Hindu, Muslim, Buddhist and you never knew Jesus Christ.

Jesus did say, 'I have come but they did not know me'. In Matthew 17;12, Jesus said;

But I tell you that Elijah has already come, and they did not recognize him, but have done to him whatever they wished. In the same way the Son of Man will suffer at their hands.

Jesus is saying, that the prophets and even himself will not be recognized by man. In my proposed idea of the Spirit Being and creation, we can deduce that mankind is under one Cosmic self, in other words one God. Whether God choose to use Mohammed, Buddha, Hindu deities is not important.

Jesus did say, 'I will bring the world unto me'.

In John 16:33,

These things I have spoken unto you, that in me ye might have peace. In the world ye shall have tribulation: but be of good cheer; I have overcome the world.

Go unto the world and make all men my disciples

In Matthew 28;19, Jesus Christ commanded his disciples to 'go unto the world and make all men my disciples'...and what do you think has happened?

Did you know that all the 12 disciples of Jesus Christ were killed? And they all rejoiced in death? The chance to die for their Master and Teacher? To deny death its victory?

The killers of the disciples did not know one very important point. The human body is not the driver of the gospel. It is the Spirit Being that drives it. By killing the human body, they free the Spirit Beings to enforce the will and memory of the Cosmos. In other words, the Galactic Memory that drives the universe. God, the Holy Spirit.

The whole world is being converted to the teachings of Christ. Not only in Jerusalem, not only in church but in the laws and courts, in the businesses and shops, in the streets and everywhere.

Just look around at Christmas. Everyone rejoice and celebrate Christmas, they don't all go to church. They are celebrating in their hearts by giving and showing love to one another where Jesus said it should be.

Why did Jesus Christ save Judaism?

We all know it was the Christians who established the State of Israel as a home for the Jewish people in 1948. Why did Jesus Christ urge his followers to save Judaism after he had destroyed Jerusalem?

The creation of the State of Israel

Here's what happened when the formal establishment of the State of Israel occurred in 1948, according to the 'Historian, Department of State, USA'.

On November 29, 1947 the United Nations adopted Resolution 181 (also known as the Partition Resolution) that would divide Great Britain's former Palestinian mandate into Jewish and Arab states in May 1948 when the British mandate was scheduled to end.

On May 14, 1948, David Ben-Gurion, the head of the Jewish Agency, proclaimed the establishment of the State of Israel. U.S. President Harry S.Truman recognized the new nation on the same day.

Note that the first mention of a Jewish home was in 1917 by the Balfour declaration, then adopted by the League of Nations in 1922, then adopted by the United Nations in 1947 (Resolution 181), then recognized by the United Nations and other nations followed….despite the opposition from the Arabs and Islam.

It should also be noted that Islam had occupied the area of Palestine for a thousand years or so, before the 1948 formalities.

We can see as we progress in this book, that all these things....or major events in history were in accordance with the Lord's prayer that Jesus taught his disciples.

Is that significant?

It would appear that the Lord's prayer is a plan for the spirit to implement....and it did happen and is happening.

I have already mentioned in my other books the significance of the creation of the State of Israel and the Vatican but let's look at it briefly.

One of the most important requirements of the New Testament is that Jesus Christ must have a historical correlation. In other words, that Jesus Christ existed in history independent of biblical accounts. Why? Because it would be proof that the books of the New Testament are authentic. It is important for our faith to be based on true stories otherwise we could be accused of false beliefs. That is very, very important for the 4 billion or so believers and followers of Christ....but also for the rest of the world where Christ has influence.

The State of Israel is the guardian of the history of Jesus Christ.

The creation of the Vatican also cements the Kingdom of God on earth. The Catholic Church is the biggest Christian Church and it is also bigger than either Hinduism and Buddhism...not counting all the other Christian Churches. The Vatican as a Sovereign State is a very big statement by Christianity....'thy Kingdom come, thy will be done on earth as it is in heaven'.

Just to emphasize the point....

In my book, 'Live a life of miracles', I discussed this very idea which is very, very important for Christianity itself.

There must be proof that Jesus Christ existed in history. All of the books of the Christian Bible's New Testament are based on historical accounts of the disciples of Jesus Christ. If there is no record of Jesus Christ in history then all the books of the New Testament are just 'fairy tales' in the eyes of its critics because Jesus Christ never existed as a man in history.

I believe that this is the very reason why Jesus Christ urged his followers to rebuild Jerusalem and let the Jews guard it with their lives. Despite their anti-Jesus Christ stance, Judaism depends on Jesus Christ for their very survival.

I believe also that this is the very reason why Islam wants to wipe Israel off the map. Israel (Judaism) does not believe in Jesus Christ. Jesus Christ is also a sacred person in Islam......but the Christians will always help Israel and allow them to defend the history of Jesus Christ.

Pope Francis, of the Catholic Church, had recently, in March 2013, held out a hand of cooperation to Islam, Judaism and other groups who took it eagerly. The historical meeting marks a new development in the work of the Holy Spirit.

Where do the Christians get their power?

In the modern world equality is now the norm with all religions and peoples on the same playing field. But in the past, you may note that the Christians and the Christian nations were the most powerful on earth in finance, in military, in wealth. There is only one reason for it. The power of the Holy Spirit....and they exhibit Christ like behavior like charity, love thy neighbour and so on. Guess who is behind it? Who is bringing all the world unto him?

All religions and even non-religious organizations preach against a 'destructive' life and promote a healthy life style.

In Christianity, a healthy life style includes lots of 'good' activities, like going to church, helping other people and reading of the Bible.

In a destructive life style, there is only 'destructive activities' which only promote behaviour that does not promote 'goodness' or development of the 'self'.

I must point out as already discussed, that all religions practice the same principles. They may differ in the details but the belief system is still the same.

To emphasize this point again.....it really does not matter what religion you belong to as long as you meet the condition as explained in example 1, in my view.

Why do non-religious people still succeed?

It is rather interesting that people who do not believe in creation, the Bible or Christianity still do live by Christian principles. They still talk about helping others, loving their neighbors, believing in themselves and others.

Some may argue that it was not Jesus Christ that first promoted the values held by Christians throughout the world. That we can find some remnants of these teachings in older religions like Hinduism and Buddhism.

Judaism is also much older than Christianity by about 2,000 years. Judaism is the religion practiced by the Jewish people. Interestingly, the old testament of the Christian Bible has its roots in Judaism and even Christianity and the teachings of Christ has some remnants in Judaism.

Judaism denies the claims of Jesus Christ and Christianity but they do admit there was a man named Jesus Christ who grew up in Nazareth whose parents were Mary and Joseph. It is this admission by Judaism that there is a historical Jesus which gives evidence and support to the authenticity of the New Testament of the Christian Bible. In addition, the writings of the apostle Paul, who was a crusader for the Jewish authorities before Christ converted him, or rather chose him to preach his gospel.

When you read the books in the new testament of the Christian Bible and understand what they mean, you can see that Jesus Christ was really who he claims to be. And therefore those values he preached were really his own.

What does that mean?

It means that if Jesus Christ is God the Son, part of the Trinity then the values he proposes that we live by is God's will. God's design for our lives.

It is those values that people uphold, whether they be religious or not, that makes the difference.

You may want to note the story of Saul. Saul was a man who was destructive. He spent his time killing and maiming good people. The Christians. And what happened to Saul? He was struck down by lightning. In Acts 9;1-19, the story of Saul is told.

What did Jesus see in Saul that he chose him to preach the gospel? He could have just burned him to ashes?

Saul did have many attributes that were lacking in his 12 disciples.

1. Saul was educated and well known in Judaism
2. Saul has Roman citizenship

Jesus knew Saul will be the perfect ambassador for the gospel and it does show that Jesus already knew Saul, who became Paul, will write 14 of the 27 books of the Christian Bible's New Testament.

Again, we can see the evidence of the power of the Holy Spirit. The description of the arrival of the Holy Spirit leaves no doubt as to who struck Saul down.

When you love thy neighbour, love your self and family, do good for others, live by the virtues of goodness you are promoting the same values of Christ.

As already mentioned...the same good and wholesome values practiced by other religions. Even in non-religious, non-educated spiritual healing, there is a

recognition of the goodness of the
Cosmic Spirit and the Cosmic self.

For example, in Hinduism and Buddhism
the older religions of Asia, the main
concern of all devotees is to escape the
sinful and painful existence of the earth
and return to God. God is described by
various identities like the Cosmic Spirit
and other names.

In that sense, there is no difference in the
main belief for salvation in all the main
religions of the world. The idea being we
are in a sinful, painful existence and we
should strive to escape this world.

Guess what is the requirement for
escaping the sinful, painful world in
Hinduism and Buddhism?

Doing good deeds! Good karma!

Exactly the same condition I have
discussed in the first example.

I have discussed this topic in many of the other books on 'God is Energy. Do you Believe?'.

The Galactic Memory

Physicists talk of the 'properties' of the universe and sub-atomic particles and if you are scientific minded, you can see the connection between creation and science. I have discussed this issue in many of my other books on religion.

What is most interesting is the idea that the memory of the Cosmos is accessible to all of us. The Galactic Memory I have spoken of many times.

Is that why the Spirit Being is in charge of our memories? Because it contributes to the Cosmic Database? If this is true then access to the Cosmic Memory where the Galactic Memory of all humans, and probably other life forms can be found, is the source of divine power and creation.

Because who else, other than God, has access to the Cosmic Memory?.

Here's another mind boggling suggestion that makes a lot of sense.

Evolution is driven by the Galactic Memory by the Galactic Database. How does that happen?

The proof of the Spirit Being also suggest that animals and plants do have a spiritual self. When animals and plants die their Spiritual self goes back to the Cosmic self the same as human spiritual beings returning to the Cosmic Spirit. The memory as already proposed is stored in the Spirit self or Spirit Being and this memory is added to the Cosmic Database.

When new life is born, the new Spirit driver brings new information to improve the new being thus divine creation evolves life on earth that way by using the memory of past lives. The proof is in some ailments that are healed by Spiritual Healers which has its causes in former lives!

Evolution is the Spirit's influence

Charles Darwin was not the first to propose evolution. There were many others like Jean Baptiste - Lamarck (1744-1829) who proposed his theory of the transmutation of species, the first fully formed theory of evolution.

Charles Darwin followed in 1858 with Alfred Russel Wallace publishing a new evolutionary theory in 'Origin of Species' (1859).

What need to be clarified is why would evolution happen by natural selection as if its all accidental? This is one interesting phenomenon of the human condition, we tend to attribute creation to random events in nature. We often forget that there are also 'non-random' events in nature.

In my book, 'The Antichrist', I talk about a 'test for non-randomness' which will help us understand that some things are not random....that it is caused by 'divine intervention' or as pointed out by 'the Galactic Cosmic Self'.

In Physics, the phenomenon of 'entanglement' suggest that it is all random and not affected by any outside force. But in Einstein's equation $E = mc^2$, it does suggest that energy can have moments of different behavior. That atoms, and particles, can change from a mass formation into an energy formation. That behavior of particles is not random but affected by energy.

In my books 'God is Energy. Do you Believe?' I have put forward some arguments that energy as already described in the Laws of Thermodynamics and Laws of Conservation of Energy has the power over everything. Which is why I propose that God is Energy. God is an

Energy Being which cannot be created or destroyed. God is omniscient and omnipotent. God controls the Galactic Database. The memory of the universe or multiverse from the beginning. I say beginning because our world exist according to time but as pointed out in Albert Einstein's theory of relativity, God exist in a timeless existence so therefore God has been there all the time but the multiverse or parts of it were created at some point in time.

It is rather difficult to believe that evolution as proposed by Charles Darwin was driven only by accidental events that causes selection pressure on living organisms and therefore only allow the 'best fit' species to survive.

In this new awakening era, where entities that live beyond death of the human body, can be proved to exist, we must find out why.

Why is it that a Spirit Being exist in the human body? Why is it that the Spirit Being survives and the human body dies? Why is it that the Spirit Being remembers events when the human body is dead?

Could it be that the selection pressure is the Galactic Cosmic Database? The source of all spiritual memory of past developments whether environmental or genetic.

The answer has been there all the time in many of the religious beliefs and Christian teachings. We are Spirit Beings in human bodies and I dare propose....that all other living organisms have spirits too!

Spiritual healing

We can now get a glimpse of the eternal corridor where we can have access to infinite power and knowledge. There are many incidences of spiritual healers whose work has been documented where they point to the 'Cosmic Memory' as the source of their power to heal. Where they find the knowledge to prescribe healing events that still amaze everybody to this day. How are they connected to the 'Cosmic Memory'?

I read a book about one such healer in the United States. He was not skilled in anything nor was he educated, but he suddenly awoke one day with the clear eyed knowledge that he has the power to heal. Many doubters tested him and found all his prescriptions to be, not only surprising, but it worked for his 'patients'.

The healer was not a religious person but he sometimes prescribe Christian Bible reading as required for the healing of some troubled people who came to seek his help....and it always worked!

The most surprising revelation, I found, was his discussion of the source of his power. He said, that it was the 'Cosmic Memory' where he gets his knowledge from. It is not a new idea either, it has some remnants in Hinduism and other religions too.

In most religions they attribute the divine power and knowledge to God or God like figures. Ancient practitioners found that they can access knowledge and power through meditation for example. Buddha is one such person.

In Christianity, prayer is a form of communication with the 'Cosmic Memory' which can only be part of God, the Trinity.

Is the Cosmic Memory that same as the Holy Spirit? It could well be that the Holy Spirit, in Christianity, which is also known as the Cosmic Spirit in religions like Hinduism is the 'Cosmic Memory' or the collective of all Spirit Beings.

Just like in our water example, you can take some of the water from the source, like a river, for your use but ultimately the water, through the water cycle will end up back in the river again. It evaporates up into the clouds then came back down in the rain. The water cycle.

Since water is conserved, you can reuse it again and again. It does suggest that as in Hinduism reincarnation proposals, that souls are being born again and again but will ultimately find their way back to the Cosmic Spirit. Just like conservation of energy as already pointed out earlier.

In our modern knowledge of religion and science, it is much easier to know more about the spirit by deduction.

Chapter 2.

Improving your spiritual existence

I often mention our 'galactic memory', in many of my other books, as something that will prove beyond a reasonable doubt that we are Spirit Beings in human bodies. Where we have been in the last billion years, is stored in the Galactic Memory, since the Spirit Being is eternal.

The problem is that, the Galactic Memory is under the control of the Spirit Being. And just like all those things that you asked for in prayer, you may not get what you want but you will always get what you need.

However, we do have glimpses of our eternal memory and knowledge when we really apply ourselves.

For example, if you discuss a plan you always know a lot of details which will not need to be explained. When you explain the trip to the supermarket, you don't talk about all the houses and traffic lights on the road or how many cars you came across or how you knew where to find the supermarket. That is all assumed because the person listening has been on that road and supermarket and knows all those details that won't need explanation. You and the other person can remember the details of the trip to the supermarket because it was you had already made the trip in this lifetime.

Suppose you were a man called John in a former life and you lived in a different country. How can you recall all of John's experience? Or even just one day and one of his trips to the supermarket? You obviously have no recollection of John or his existence in that former life.

What does that mean?

Suppose you also lived during the time of Jesus Christ, but you have no recollection of that lifetime.

What does that mean?

It means, you are not in control of the 'Galactic Memory'. It is the Spirit Being that controls your Galactic Memory. Man's collective memory from the very beginning.

How I can I prove that?

In millions of OBEs (out of body experience) and NDEs (near death experience) individuals who went through these experiences relate their stories which suggest that there is an entity that live on after death of the human body.

In all cases, the dead person seem to recall what happened to them when they were dead. They were able to describe the people and activities as well as their surroundings in great detail. They were watching what was going on from outside their dead body! Even though they have been pronounced dead by the Doctors!

When these individuals wake up from the dead, they can recall everything! They even said, they were watching their dead bodies from above, to the amazement of all involved!

The evidence is very clear that memory actually is under the control of the Spirit Being. The entity that is still alive when the human body is already pronounced dead by the Doctors.

There are numerous cases of spiritual healing where the healer himself/herself was under some 'spiritual guidance' and who never really practice religion or go to church as mentioned in the previous chapter.

It does appear that the power to heal is from an entity in 'collaboration' with the healer. It confirms that Spirit Beings do intercede and help humans from time to time. As one of the healers related, the power to heal, in such a case, comes from the Cosmos. I propose it is the Galactic Memory where all the knowledge is stored.

There are millions of cases of spiritual healing and spiritual intervention on record. Records of NDE and OBE is just one area of spiritual existence evident in its prolific happenings.

It also does seem that when a spirit returns to the Cosmic Spirit, it merges with it perhaps downloading its memory content to the Cosmic reservoir or as already mentioned Cosmic Memory. This may explain why you cannot recall your previous lives because your past memories are already filed in the Cosmic Memory.

For example, using our water example again, you can take water from a muddy river and use it but the water evaporating will not have any of the contents that made it muddy. So the rain that falls, with the amount of water you took from the muddy river, will not have any 'muddy content'....being your memory.

The muddy content remains in the soil or has gone back to the earth!

The Holy Spirit

Jesus Christ did point out in Matthew 28:20

'I will always be with you even to the end of the world'

This is one piece of evidence that Jesus Christ has already come. He is the Holy

Spirit who arrived on Pentecost and he will be here to the end of the world.

I have discussed this in many of my other books.

I have no doubt that what is happening on earth, as has happened already in the past 2,000 years, is the work of the Holy Spirit. There is no other explanation for it.

How can we have a relationship with the Holy Spirit?

I like to use one of the verses that prompted the book 'The Antichrist', it is a verse from the apostle 1 John 4:4,

'the one inside you is stronger than the one out there'

What John is saying is that those who have accepted Jesus Christ as their Lord and Savior has already got the Holy Spirit. Just like the Holy Spirit entered the apostles on Pentecost and enabled them to become like Christ, to perform miracles in his name.

Discovering the spirit

We have discussed the issue of memory. The evidence is clear, the spirit controls the memory. You will be surprised that the spirit also controls the emotion.

In the example of my son telling me to stop smoking at age 7, there is a very important observation there. I felt the little boy was very sincere about it. His new found knowledge at school that smoking is bad suddenly gave him motivation to stop his Dad from smoking. He does not want anything bad to happen to his Daddy....and he won't give up. He repeatedly lectured me on the teachers view that smoking is bad. I suddenly felt the kid is right, something really deep down inside just clicked I suddenly lost ALL desire to smoke cigarettes.

If you have been a smoker for 30 years, you know it is very difficult to quit. Smoking is very addictive. Most people will go through a period of withdrawl. They chew gum or take 'patches' of nicotine attached to the skin to stop their cravings for a cigarette. In my case, I just suddenly lost all my desire to smoke. Just thinking about smoking made me feel sick.

I realized that the decision to quit smoking was not made by the human. It was the spirit that made the decision. The little kid awakened the emotion and appealed to the spirit that he does not want his Daddy to get sick from smoking. And the spirit heard him and stopped the human from smoking in an instant.

I related this experience in my ebook 'Quit smoking in 2 seconds' (amazon.com), I felt that was how long it took the spirit to stop me from smoking. The spirit can detect the little kid's love for his Daddy, the emotion of it.

I believe that is what happened. I don't need to chew gum or use nicotine patches, the spirit just changed my thinking and reversed all my desires to smoke.

That also raises the question of desire. It does seem that the emotions is linked to the desires. This is also controlled by the spirit.

That is a very important point in our spirituality. Realization is a key here, understanding that our memory, emotions and desires are controlled by the spirit suddenly puts things in perspective. If you want to make changes in your life, you must recruit or appeal to the spirit to make the change. The human cannot do it.

It also raises another question. What is the relationship between emotion and thoughts? It seems that emotion follows the thought process. Emotion is the product of the thought process.

What is thought? Or thinking?

Our thinking is affected by our visual and audio senses. What you see and hear. Now we can link them. It does seem that your thoughts and senses are also controlled by the spirit.

This is the message of Jesus Christ. In order for us to be saved, we must save the spirit. There is no point saving the human, he is destined to return to the earth. That is why being good is a precondition for success as explained in Example 1. The spirit is good. In order for the spirit to perform the human must also be good. It does suggest that having good karma is a very good idea.

If the spirit controls memory, emotions, thoughts, feelings then what does the human control? Surely, it is the spirit that is in charge. It does seem that the human has influence on several levels. The sensory inputs, or what we see and hear, and physical inputs. By physical inputs I mean food, drink, drugs and so on.

That is why the spirit wants to stop me from smoking and drinking alcohol, it is not necessary for me to do those things. In fact, they are destructive to the human body.

There is certainly some truth to the Bible notion that our body is God's temple and we must look after it as best we could.

If the aim of the human is improving his karma, then surely the spirit would be happier returning to the Cosmic Spirit as soon as possible? Terminating the human existence as soon as practicable? It does appear that the spirit is protecting the human and preserving the human for as long as possible.

What is the purpose of preserving the weak and problematic human?

Why was the human created in the first place?

If we grow potatoes for food we have to do certain things. First we prepare the soil and add fertilizer, then plant the potatoes. Once the potato plants start growing we spray it, with chemicals, to protect against disease and insects. We water it to improve its growth. After about 4 months or so when the potatoes are mature then we harvest it and store it for future food.

Being a human is like the potato crop. We would not harvest it before it matures. We only harvest the potatoes when they are ready. Similarly, the spirit would not terminate the human until he is ready. We would not harvest the potatoes at 2 months because they are not mature and no one will buy or eat them, we have to wait till they are 4 months and mature.

That gives us a glimpse of the purpose. The purpose of creation. The Spirit Being is being cultivated in the human, the temple of God, and is only harvested or returns to the Cosmic Spirit when it is mature. Does that mean that the spirit feeds the Galactic Memory? To keep it alive and powerful?

It does appear to be so.

Our existence is a creation like a potato field. No wonder Jesus Christ used the parable of the man and his vineyard to describe the human condition. We are like the vineyard or the potatoes, we are a creation or cultivation of God.

Our spiritual existence gives the Cosmic self its power. It should be pointed out that the seed of the spirit came from the Cosmos in the first place, and once its life on earth is complete it goes back.

I like to think of the spirit as like water in the water cycle. It falls down as rain from the sky, it turns in to ice in the cold but

when its hot it evaporates as water
vapour and return to the sky.

The Spirit Being is made up of photons!

Physicists say that photons store within
their electromagnetic oscillations what
had transpired in the past to even billions
of years ago. What is even more amazing
is that a photon is described as the
'energy released when an electron jumps
from a high energy orbit to a lower
energy orbit in the atom'. And these
photons can be collected and studied!
There are quite a large amount of it just
zooming around in space!

If we can deduce the past from the
electromagnetic records on the photon
then we can now get a glimpse of what
'The Spirit Beings' are made of.

I have often referred to the Spirit Being as
the 'Energy Being'. Now we know for sure
that they are spirit beings! We also know
now that the Energy Being or Spirit Being

is released as photons when a person dies! The electrons which were circulating at high energy levels suddenly zips down to level zero and all the energy or photons are released…..as the Energy Being.

We also know why the Spirit Being controls the memory! Its in the electromagnetic record of its photon self! And now we can define death in energy terms;

Death in a human being is a state where all its energy have been released as electromagnetic photons

We now know why the dead can be raised in the hospitals. The electric currents just gives the dead body a new set of photons to charge up its electrons and get them to start orbiting!

Would you say that if the electrons are excited we will get a higher spiritual experience?

If our memory reside in the electromagnetic spectrum of the photon and photons will survive forever then we can safely assume that if we work out how to control our photon output we could control life itself! We should remember that photons are packets or quanta of energy which cannot be destroyed!

In theory, if the photons contain the memory of the universe then we can assume that the sun contains all the photons that come into earth.

Does that mean our collective memory is in the sun?

But what about those that leave the earth? Science predicts that photons cannot be destroyed but can only be changed into other forms of energy. If the memory in the Spirit Being are made of electromagnetic oscillations then what does it change into? Science also suggest that photons are absorbed into atoms where they energize the electrons to become excited.   Note the photon has zero mass, so according to Albert Einsteins famous equation $E = mc^2$ when mass is zero, energy equals the square of the velocity of light.

What does that mean?

It means that energy equals the value of the light intensity. In other words, energy and light are the same thing!

We are back to the photon definition!

In terms of the existence of the Spirit Being when mass is absent, energy will exist as light! Exactly what the photon is.

Which brings us to the question. When does light becomes mass?

The Sun is the star of our solar system

Science proposes that the sun make up 99.8 % of the mass of the solar system. It is made up of 70% hydrogen and 28% helium with a 865,000 kilometer diameter. Its weight or mass is most likely from the helium and there are 1.4×10^{27} cubic meters in the sun. We are talking about a huge, huge volume. For example, about 1.3 million earths will fit inside the sun. One cubic metre of helium weighs about 900 kilograms. The massive mass of the sun gives it its very strong gravity.

The energy given off by the sun comes from the constant fusion of hydrogen to form helium. It takes 4 hydrogen nuclei to produce two positrons, two neutrinos, two gamma-ray photons, and a helium-4 nucleus. A gamma-ray photon is typically defined in astrophysics as having 100 keV (kiloelectron volts) or more. Those less than 100 keV are known as x rays. Gamma-ray photons are the most powerful and energetic of the electron magnetic spectrum. They are emitted by 'excited' states of the atom.

All the light on earth comes from the sun, apart from man made electricity. This light is the energy emitted by the fusion of hydrogen to form helium. We can tell it is a huge amount as we can feel its heat 93 million miles away on earth.

How is the light produced?

This is exactly what $E = mc^2$ predicted. When energy is emitted as photons, which has zero mass, energy exist as light!

What happens to the endless stream of rays coming from the sun?

The gamma and harmful rays are absorbed by the earth's atmosphere. Only a small fraction of the photons from the sun reaches the earth. It is these photons of energy that plants use for their own life processes and production of carbohydrates, proteins and other vitamins and trace elements which sustain life on earth.

As earlier mentioned, photons from stars millions of light years away which reach the earth do contain the 'memory' of its travels in its electromagnetic spectrum.

What does it all mean?

Are photons the vehicle of the Gods?

We have already discussed the possibility that photons emitted by the human body forms the entity I have named the Spirit Being. When these photons are released the electrons of the human body cease to function and the human body dies. Because photon is energy, it cannot be destroyed. Thus by extrapolation, the Spirit Being is eternal.

We have discussed that the Spirit Being has an electromagnetic component which stores the memory of its entire existence.

Here's the amazing conclusion to our discussion so far;

1. The Spirit Being is made of energy called photons emitted by the atoms of the human body
2. The Spirit Being is eternal
3. The Spirit Being has zero mass because photons has zero mass
4. Because it has zero mass, the Spirit Being exist as light
5. Light does not have a beginning or end, time does not exist (which is why the Spirit Being is eternal!)
6. The Spirit Being is light and it moves at the speed of 300,000 km/second
7. Light that arrives on earth may possibly bring Spirit Beings from other stars in the universe

I wonder why they called Jesus Christ the 'Light of the World'?

Chapter 3.

The work of the Spirit Being

You may ask, why is it that the Spirit Being need a human body? If it can exist for eternity by itself then why exist in pain and suffering as a human?

Most humans would not choose to exist in a lower form of life so it would appear contradictory that a human body is disposable from the point of view of the spirit.

In my example when discussing the Trinity, in my 'God is Energy. Do you Believe? series of books, I used the example of water to illustrate how God can exist in three persons. God the Father, God the Son and God the Holy Ghost just like the water can exist as ice, liquid and vapour or gas.

But in that example of water we can also see the difference in the 3 states. The key to the existence of each state of water depends on its energy or the energy applied to it.

When heat is applied to ice it becomes a liquid add more heat and it becomes a gas like vapour.

Does the human body and spirit being states behave in the same way? What are the conditions for the Spirit Being to leave the human body?

I have also given the example of Albert Einstein's equation $E = mc^2$ where Einstein points out that matter and energy are interchangeable. In other words the human body can also become energy. In the case of the atomic bomb, for example, a small amount of solid is released into energy in a split second thus creating so much power and devastation. Unfortunately for our human example, it seems that the energy, the spirit, can be released but without the body exploding or disappearing.

Perhaps its just a partial release of energy?

What then is the work of the Spirit Being and why there is a need for a body?

We have discussed in the previous chapter that The Spirit Being can also be described in the behavior of photons, which is energy released by electrons moving from higher to lower levels of energy or orbits. And the mind boggling realization that because photons have zero mass they can only exist as light energy.

We have established that the memory is controlled by the Spirit Being. So if that is the case then we have a clue to its purpose.

In Albert Einstein's theory of relativity it is suggested that when you approach the speed of light, time slows down and cease to exist.

It is also suggested that you can travel to the future and the past ...and Physicists suggest that it is the 'memory of the universe' where you can, which have been discovered to be stored in the electromagnetic portion of photons.

Apparently everything that happens in the universe or multiverse is recorded in the memory of the universe. Just like how we can predict the decay of radioactive material so we can trace it back to its original state.

Note that the memory is stored in the electromagnetic spectrum of light or photons and it is not static. It moves at 300,000 km/second.

Note these are Physicists who explain that it is quite possible to travel through time and also enter into new dimensions and parallel universes. Not so different from what religions have been preaching for centuries.

Eureka!.....and we have found it! The photons or light energy stores the memory of its existence! Therefore, the Spirit Being, as already mentioned, controls the memory of the self. In addition, to the memory of the cosmos. The Galactic Memory.

Photons of light energy

We have already discussed that photons of light from the sun helps plants to produce the food that sustains the earth. All the food we eat has its original value and content in plants.

In my book series 'God is Energy. Do you Believe?', I already proposed that God is Energy and it makes sense.

Here are the conclusions so far;

1. God is Energy
2. Energy also exist as light
3. Light helps plants to make food for the earth
4. Light as photons stores the memory of the cosmos
5. Light illuminate what we humans can see, without light we cannot see anything
6. Light can travel throughout the universe
7. Light may be the 'mode of travel' for Spirit Beings
8. Energy can be transferred to other forms to create work
9. Work on earth will cease without energy
10. Energy is transferred in light

The more we continue with this discussion, the more we realize that everything in the universe and multiverse may be connected!

Dark matter

Dark matter is a theoretical force opposite gravity which causes the universe to expand at an accelerating rate. It is the most common material in the universe being constant in its presence, accounting for 85% of all the matter in the universe but only 27 % of its mass. There is a suggestion it is made of protons, neutrons and electrons.

And dark matter emits dark photons which are relatively massive particles! If light photons are the Spirit Beings then what is the dark photons? Dark photons, unlike its light counterpart, is still a theoretical particle in the same boat as antimatter.

The theory is that, all matter has a corresponding antimatter. For example, an electron's antimatter counterpart would be a positron.

What is clear is that, just like a magnet it seems that antimatter is necessary to hold everything together because like charges oppose each other. In other words matter and matter will not stick together.

Does dark matter explain why there is an opposite of God?

In my book, 'The Antichrist', I proposed that the Antichrist is not a man but the Polar Opposite of God. Like everything in the universe, it does appear that antimatter is necessary to hold the universe together.

But is it necessary to have an Antichrist? Does having an Antichrist define the existence of Christ?

Does the existence of the dark photon give more description and meaning to the light photon. At this stage, the dark photon is just a theory but the idea and proposal is there.

If the light photons can explain the existence of the Spirit Being then does the dark photon explain the existence of the devil?

It would appear that according to the knowledge we have now the devil does not exist, in other words the dark photon cannot be proved at this stage.

Then what is the devil? Who is Satan?

Satan cannot be explained by our knowledge of the physical world. That is, there is no proof although it is hypothesized.

This brings up a very, very important point. God never created a Satan in the sense of man's creation. Satan or Lucifer was an angel who disobeyed God!

No wonder we cannot explain Satan using our knowledge of the physical world. This is where we can explain why there are negative energies out there even though they were created as 'photons of light'.

Negative energy or Satan can only be explained in the Galactic Memory or Database of the Cosmos. As we have already seen, in the past discussions, sometimes negative memories of past events can cause disabilities in the present!

For example, Spiritual Healers who can heal sick or disabled individuals just by prescribing Christian Bible verses for them to read and they are healed!

There are two amazing events that occurred in this kind of healing. Firstly, it proves and demonstrates that the Spirit Being is the cause of the disability because it holds the memory of past lives and events. Secondly, it proves the authenticity of Jesus Christ because the Spirit Being accepts the words of the Christian Bible New Testament has healing powers. In other words, the Spirit

Being is healed by the words of Jesus Christ! And this healing is transferred to the human body....when the patient recovers!

There is no other explanation as to why this happens or occurs with spiritual healers.

Chapter 4.

Technology and Evidence

Would you say that a machine has intelligence?

For example, a car. It can move faster than you, carry a lot more people than you and do a lot of things that you cannot do. In that sense, clearly a car is far superior than a mere weakling like a human. But it was the human that made the car and give it also those powerful attributes. We all know that the car engine works because of the battery and electrical system.

What about the human?

The human heart, for example, beats because there is a tiny little transistor like battery in one corner of it. It emits little electrical pulses that contracts the heart and pump the blood that gives your body life giving oxygen. Not so different from a car.

So what makes the human different? What makes the human intelligent? A car like a dead human body, can sit in the garage and will do nothing. It is only when you start the engine that it roars into life.

Likewise, the dead human body has all its parts intact but it will not do anything until you put life into it. For example, in the hospitals where Doctors can revive dead patients with electrical pulses to restart the heart. Not so different from the car.

I have put forward the explanation, in the previous chapters, that the photons of energy maybe the key here. When the photon of energy is lost it can be replaced by electric energy.

In NDE and OBE accounts it does appear that when the human body is dead the Spirit Being has moved outside the body. In my series of books called 'God is Energy. Do you Believe?' I explored this phenomenon with the available evidence. Apparently the energy required to start the car, which comes from the battery, is the same energy that is required to revive a human which comes from a battery called the 'defibrillator'.

In the car example, there is an added factor, the driver. The driver must be there to drive the car. Otherwise like the dead human body, the car is going nowhere. Also in the human, the Spirit Being must be there to drive the human body. Isn't that an excellent deduction? That without the Spirit Being the human body, just like the car, will remain dead.

This deduction is supported by OBE and NDE observation, that the entity which makes the observation from outside the body while it is announced dead by the Doctors, is the Spirit Being that drives the body.

It does give a lot of power to the words of Christ in John 10:10;

'I have come so that you may have life, and have it abundantly'

In my series of books, 'God is Energy. Do you Believe?', I tried to present the case that God is energy. Not only it is supported by scientific laws but also by observation.

Let's look at three scientific laws or observations that help explain God.

Example 1.

The first law of thermodynamics also known as the Law of Conservation of Energy

This law states that energy can neither be created nor destroyed. Energy can only be transferred or changed from one form to another.

For example, turning on a light would seem to produce energy; however, it is electrical energy that is converted.

The description of God in the Christian Bible explains that God was not created and cannot be destroyed. It is the omniscience and omnipotent qualities of God that make him all knowing and all powerful.

In the Christian Bible, it is also suggested in the story of Adam and Eve, in the book of Genesis that Adam was made in the image of God. There is a suggestion in the story that Adam must have been an immortal Spirit Being but was turned into a mortal, together with Eve, as punishment for their disobedience.

Example 2.

Albert Einsteins equation $E = mc^2$

Albert Einstein's equation proves that mass and energy are interchangeable but the key ingredient is the speed of light. There are various points here that give us a clue to the nature of God.

(i) If mass and energy are interchangeable then this is scientific evidence that you can appear and disappear like angels do in the Christian Bible. We just don't know how it works yet but this is scientific proof that angels or even Jesus Christ appearing and disappearing is not fiction or fairy tales but have a scientific basis.

Hollywood has already used this discovery in many movies. 'Star Trek' being the most obvious one where the crew of the spacecraft can be 'beamed anywhere' in the universe!

(ii) The other point to note is that the speed of light which is a function of distance over time, gives us an amazing insight. Suppose you travel to some other planet and as you approach the speed of light, time slows down and come to a stop. In other words, when you experience the state of travelling at the speed of light, time does not exist. This is an amazing phenomenon described by Albert Einstein's theory of relativity.

It does mean that in God's 'world', time does not exist and so it is possible to live forever because there is no time. I have already discussed this point relating to the Spirit Beings. If they exist as photons, which has no mass, they can only exist as light or energy.....and time does not exist.

It does mean also that in our human world we age according to time because we are made of mass and mass is subject to time decay.

Many of the eminent physicists today talk of a multiverse or many universes all packed together like several trays of eggs on each other but without the trays. The eggs lying on their sides would be the universes in this multiverse. We also refer to them as dimensions.

It does appear that the 'timeless state' has to do with the 'energy state' of God. Because at the speed of light the mass changes into energy. It follows that to have a timeless existence we must leave our human body because the human body, as mass, ages with time.

The Spirit Being exist in an energy state where time does not exist. They exist as light energy, brilliantly described by the behavior of photons.

Chapter 5.

Where do the fossils fit in?

One of the reasons why many people do not believe the Christian Bible is that, it does not account for many historical facts like the fossil record, for example.

That is where evolution has a clear advantage.

We now know that there were global disasters in the past which had wiped out life on earth. The dinosaurs became extinct 65 million years ago after living on earth for 165 million years. The most popular theory was a comet had hit earth and the explosion, and its effects, was big enough to wipe out the dinosaurs and many other plants and animals.

Then there was, what the historians and archaeologists call the 'deluge' which is basically Noah's flood, which destroyed all living animals of the time. I suppose only those rescued by Noah survived.

The critics argue that the Christian Bible accounts suggest that the earth as we know it now is only 6,000 years old. Science has pointed out that the earth is closer to 5 billion years old. I say 5 billion because that is the age of our sun and science predicts there is only another 5 billion years before the sun runs out of its 10 billion year fuel load.

One of the points that should be cleared first is that the Christian Bible were written by men of those ages and it reflects their knowledge of the world. However, more and more theories are emerging of some of the 'visions recorded in the Bible' which are now thought to be communications with extra-terrestrials. There is another book which is not included in the Bible with many stories out of this world. The book of Enoch for example, the 7th generation from Adam.

The oldest *Homo sapiens* fossil found by anthropologists is about 315,000 years old. There are some fossils which are much older, closer to 2 million years which are supposedly called the ancestors of *Homo sapiens*, *Homo habilis* for example.

What does that mean in terms of Biblical accounts?. Well, it does not mean anything. We have to accept that the Christian Bible is a spiritual guide and not a history of the world. The Bible does not have accounts of much of scientific records of the fossil evolution and development of technology. Similarly, the Christian Bible does not tell us about the planetary universe or the multiverse now proposed by science.

What the Bible is telling us is what we need to know about ourselves. Apparently, there is another world that is not accounted for by the fossil record. The world of the Spirit Beings. The Christian Bible is showing us the way, how we can understand this world of the spirit.

This is a very, very important consideration in terms of man's existence on the earth. First we know that we have no control over the earth or the solar system or the universe but we are learning the laws that govern it.

Suddenly we stumble over some new realization that our scientific knowledge can help us understand the unseen world of the spirit.

Some theories now suggest that there is evidence from the Bible that God had destroyed life on earth many times because he does not like the animals that emerged from his creation.

The stories of the giant Nephilim, in the Bible, for example. The giant Nephilims were the sons of the 'children of God' and mortal women.

In the fossil records around the world there are giant humans so big that modern humans are only as tall as the smallest finger on the giant's hand. The heights of these super humans range from 8 feet to more than 30 feet high according to various accounts! It is also interesting that much of this fossil record has largely been ignored by science.

The fossil record is full of many weird and wonderful skeletons, some of which begs explanation. It does mean that the earth had suffered catastrophes many times which has wiped out many of those species as already happened with the dinosaurs. Five billion years is a long time. Many fossils may have disappeared completely.

Considering the new evidence of the existence of the Spirit Being, all the fossil evidence does not mean much apart from telling us that there were such animals and plants that existed in the past.

What we should be doing now is investigate the Spirit Being and how it works for us. The Christian Bible and other religious literature have already pointed out the existence of the Spirit Beings but the scientific evidence wakes us up to the realization that it is possible to discover more.

I have proposed in the previous chapters and other books that the Spirit Being is the self which drives our everyday lives. When the human body dies, the Spirit Being returns to the Cosmic Spirit. This has been pointed out by all religions.

What science has discovered from the evidence of the OBE and DNE, is that the memory may be controlled by the Spirit Being. We have evidence from Spiritual

Healers that the universe has a memory too! What I call the Galactic Memory.

It is very possible that when the Spirit Being return to the Cosmic Spirit their memory is stored in the Galactic Memory, a Galactic Database where all knowledge of everything comes from. That is where the Spiritual Healers claim their power to heal and knowledge come from.

Its not a new idea, Hinduism has a very similar concept.

In our water example of the Trinity, it is easy to see how water can exist in 3 states. It is still water but can also exist as ice and steam or vapour.

Suppose the Galactic Memory is like a Great Lake where all the water from the rivers flow. Just like the Spirit Beings are compelled to return to the Cosmic Spirit upon death of the human body. From the Great Lake water vapour can escape under the heat of the sun, similarly Spirit

Beings can take on a different form by moving out of the Galactic Memory. They can become human for example. The Great Lake can also freeze and similarly the Galactic Memory will have a period of hibernation or rest from all the activities in the multiverse.

Didn't God rest on the 7th day from all his creation work?

Is the multiverse controlled by the Galactic Memory?

We know from computer software that in order for it to work we must input the programme of instructions of how it should operate. Similarly, for the multiverse to work there must be software telling it how to behave. This must be the purpose of the Galactic Database. It is the very reason why everything evolve because new information added to the Galactic Database from new entries via the Spirit returnees can change how the multiverse behaves.

Similarly, the genetic code changes with every generation because of what the Spirit Being is experiencing. How the thoughts and experiences of the Spirit as a human is recorded and influences the genetic code and future generations processes.

I have briefly touched on this topic in the first book of 'God is Energy. Do you Believe?

I am proposing that prayer, affirmations, thoughts and activities do influence our genes and how information is recorded for future use. The proof is that in breeding programme of animals or plants, you can amplify the desired traits like bigger muscles and meat in cattle or bigger and sweeter fruits in plants simply by crossing these plants that have them.

In humans we often remark on how our children resemble their relatives in appearance and behavior which suggest that, at least some of these, inherited traits were not passed on from the ancestors!

Could they have been mutations? Probably not, and very unlikely.

Where does this influence come from?

Thoughts and memory are intertwined and possible sources of this genetic change. Especially the memory.....and we know, from our discussions in this book, who controls the memory.

About the author….

Semisi Pule, also known as Semisi Pule Pone, writes in many genre including religion. His latest books on religion is an attempt to explain religion using our scientific knowledge. This book especially looks at the possibility that the actions of light at subatomic levels can tell us a lot about our existence. It is very possible that the Spirit Beings which were first raised in the Christian Bible and other religions are very much alive and a part and parcel of human existence. Man has always known he has a spirit or soul but he did not know how to explain why it existed. More and more evidence of NDE and OBE accounts point us directly at the existence of an entity that live on beyond death of the human body. The Spirit Being.

As we understand a little bit more about the words of the Christian Bible, and even the teachings of other religions, we understand more about our existence and our relationship with the spirit or soul.

What is the purpose of it all?

Why do the eternal spirits need a weak and disposable human body?

I propose that the memory of the human, stored in the electromagnetic spirit, is the key. Somehow the memory of all our human thoughts, events, activities is required by the cosmos for its development. Once we die this memory is downloaded to the Galactic Memory of the universe where it joins other trillions of pieces of information linking everything together like a software operating a computer, driving evolution

of the human, animals, plants, other
living organisms and the multiverse itself.

www.ingramcontent.com/pod-product-compliance
Lightning Source LLC
LaVergne TN
LVHW051353080426
835509LV00020BB/3413